W9-AQB-320

Date: 3/22/13

J 597.928 FRA
Franchino, Vicky.
Sea turtles /

SEA TURTLES

by Vicky Franchino

Children's Press®

An Imprint of Scholastic Inc.
New York   Toronto   London   Auckland   Sydney
Mexico City   New Delhi   Hong Kong
Danbury, Connecticut

Content Consultant
Dr. Stephen S. Ditchkoff
Professor of Wildlife Sciences
Auburn University
Auburn, Alabama

Photographs © 2013: age fotostock: 1, 15 (Gerald Nowak/
imagebro), 19 (MarkDoh); Alamy Images: 23 (David Santiago
Garcia/Westend61 GmbH), 39 (Melinda Podor), 11 (Michael
Patrick O'Neill), cover (Reinhard Dirscherl); Bob Italiano: 44
foreground, 45 foreground; Corbis Images/Â Kike Calvo/Retna:
31; Dreamstime: 5 top, 35 (Christopher Howey), 12 (Gents), 16
(Marjanvisserphotography), 2 background, 3 background, 44
background, 45 background (Tatiana Belova);
Getty Images: 4, 5 background, 20
(Jason Isley - Scubazoo), 28 (Rene
Frederick), 32 (Tim Zurowski/All
Canada Photos); Kat Franchino:
48; Photo Researchers/B. G.
Thomson: 24; Shutterstock, Inc.:
2 foreground, 3 foreground, 7, 46
(idreamphoto), 36 (Ryan M. Bolton); Superstock, Inc.: 40
(Eye Ubiquitous), 5 bottom, 8 (Fleetman/VWPics), 27
(Mark Conlin/VWPics).

Library of Congress Cataloging-in-Publication Data
Franchino, Vicky.
  Sea turtles / by Vicky Franchino.
      pages cm.–(Nature's children)
  Includes bibliographical references and index.
  Audience: Ages 9–12.
  Audience: Grades 4–6.
  ISBN 978-0-531-20981-3 (lib. bdg.)
  ISBN 978-0-531-24307-7 (pbk.)
  1. Sea turtles–Juvenile literature. I. Title.
  QL666.C536F726 2013
  597.92'8–dc23   2012034331

1 2 3 4 5 6 7 8 9 10 R 22 21 20 19 18 17 16 15 14 13

Sea Turtles

Class	Reptilia
Order	Testudines
Families	Cheloniidae and Dermochelyidae
Genera	6 genera
Species	7 species
World distribution	All continents except Antarctica
Habitat	Typically found in shallow coastal waters, bays, creeks, and streams; juveniles may be found at sea
Distinctive physical characteristics	All except the leatherback have a hard, protective shell; all have four flippers that they use to swim quickly through the water; cannot pull their heads or limbs into their shells; have a hard, spiky jaw; do not have teeth
Habits	Usually live on their own; only come together to travel to nesting grounds or to mate; spend much of their time underwater; must return to the surface to breathe
Diet	Some are herbivores that eat only plant life or carnivores that eat only meat; others are omnivores that eat both plants and animals

SEA TURTLES

Contents

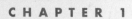

CHAPTER 1

Huge Reptiles

A seabird glides through the sky on a warm, sunny day, searching the ocean waters for a place to land. Eventually, it spots a wide, round object on the surface and swoops down to rest. It is a large flatback turtle, floating and enjoying the warmth of the sunlight. The seabird lands on the turtle's back. Together, the bird and the turtle drift along with the gentle ocean waves. Because the turtle is likely to be floating for quite a while, the bird has plenty of time to rest its wings.

Sea turtles spend almost their entire lives in the water. Many live in warm tropical oceans. Others can survive the colder temperatures of the far north and south. All sea turtles are reptiles. They are cold-blooded. This means the temperature of their body changes with the temperature of the air or water around them. Their skin is scaly. It helps keep their bodies from drying out when they are on land. Sea turtles are also vertebrates.

Sea turtles rarely leave the water.

Natural Protection

Adult sea turtles' only natural **predators** are sharks and killer whales. This is mostly because of the turtle's protective shell. The shell is part of the turtle's skeleton. The top part is the carapace. It is attached to the turtle's backbone and ribs. The underside is the plastron. The shell is made up of dozens of connected bones. The shell has **nerve** endings. This means a sea turtle can feel when something touches it.

The carapace is covered with a protective layer of **scutes**. Each turtle **species** has a different number and pattern of scutes.

There are openings in a turtle's shell for its head, tail, and legs. The only sea turtle that does not have a hard shell is the leatherback. It gets its name from its leathery shell.

FUN FACT! Scientists can estimate a sea turtle's age by examining its shell. Many have growth rings that are similar to those of a tree.

A turtle's shell is its best defense against enemies.

Seven Species

Sea turtles rarely return to land after birth. This makes it hard for scientists to know exactly how many there are. They do know that there are seven sea turtle species living in oceans and waterways around the world. The Kemp's ridley is one of the smallest. It usually doesn't grow much longer than 2 feet (0.6 meters) and weighs 100 pounds (45 kilograms) or less. Most Kemp's ridley turtles live in warm waters, but some have been found as far north as Nova Scotia and Newfoundland.

The olive ridley is another small sea turtle. It can be up to 2.5 feet (0.8 m) long. It usually weighs between 80 and 110 pounds (36 and 50 kg). This turtle gets its name from the olive color of its shell. It prefers warm water.

The flatback turtle only **breeds** in northern Australia. It gets its name from its flat, thin shell. This turtle grows to be about 3.3 feet (1 m) long. It usually weighs less than 275 pounds (125 kg).

The Kemp's ridley is smaller than most other sea turtles.

Giants of the Turtle Family

The hawksbill turtle has a beak like a hawk's. It is usually about 2.5 feet (0.8 m) long and weighs between 95 and 165 pounds (43 and 75 kg).

The loggerhead turtle's head is large compared to its body. This turtle weighs about 250 pounds (113 kg) on average. It is usually around 3 feet (0.9 m) long. It lives in ocean waters that are warm or mild in temperature.

The green sea turtle is found in shallow waters in tropical and subtropical areas. It can grow to be 4 feet (1.2 m) long and weigh more than 500 pounds (227 kg). It gets its name from the color of its body fat.

The leatherback is the largest sea turtle. This species can be up to 8 feet (2.4 m) long and can weigh up to 2,000 pounds (907 kg). It has been found as far south as Argentina and as far north as the British Isles.

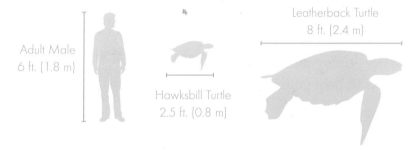

Adult Male
6 ft. (1.8 m)

Hawksbill Turtle
2.5 ft. (0.8 m)

Leatherback Turtle
8 ft. (2.4 m)

Loggerhead turtles get their name from their enormous heads.

CHAPTER 2

At Home in the Sea

Sea turtles can weigh hundreds of pounds, but they are graceful and fast swimmers. Some can swim at speeds greater than 20 miles (32 kilometers) per hour. Sea turtles have four flippers instead of feet. A turtle's front flippers help it move quickly through the water. The back flippers help it to steer.

Young sea turtles often live farther away from land than adults do. They hide in floating masses of weeds to avoid being eaten by predators. Adult sea turtles can protect themselves and often prefer coastal areas where it is easier to find food. Most adult sea turtles only go into deep water while **migrating**. Some travel thousands of miles in search of food or a place to nest.

How does a sea turtle find its way in the ocean? Many scientists believe that sea turtles have a special kind of internal compass to help guide them.

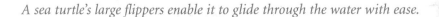

A sea turtle's large flippers enable it to glide through the water with ease.

Valuable Senses

Sea turtles rely on their senses to stay safe and locate food. They don't have ears on the outside of their head. Instead their eardrums are covered with skin. Sea turtles have a bone in their middle ear that helps them feel **vibrations** in the water. Changes in vibrations let sea turtles know if another animal is nearby.

Sea turtles have good eyesight underwater. They have large eyelids that protect their eyes. They also have a special **gland** that produces sticky tears. These tears protect the sea turtle's eyes when it is not in the water.

Smell is a sea turtle's strongest sense. In fact, sea turtles might be able to smell even better than dogs can. Scientists believe that a sea turtle smells by bringing water in through its nose and then exhaling it through its mouth. It uses this incredible ability to find food and locate nearby enemies.

Sea turtles can see farther and more clearly underwater than they can above the surface.

Toothless Turtles

A sea turtle has a hard beak similar to that of a bird. This strong beak helps the sea turtle catch and hold on to food. Different species have different types of jaws. The green sea turtle has jaws with **serrated** edges that cut through the grass it likes to eat. A loggerhead turtle has strong jaws. They crush the shells of the crabs, shrimp, and other animals that make up its diet.

There are no teeth inside a sea turtle's mouth. Its mouth and throat are lined with sharp spikes instead. These spikes keep food from escaping. They also cut the food into smaller pieces that the turtle can swallow.

Different sea turtles have different diets. Some sea turtles are herbivores. This means they only eat plants. Others are carnivores. They only eat meat. Some are omnivores. They eat a variety of plants and animals. The leatherback turtle is a carnivore. It eats jellyfish and other soft animals. It dives deep into the ocean to find its favorite meal.

Green sea turtles enjoy eating plants from the ocean floor.

Deep Breathing

Sea turtles need to breathe air. They cannot stay submerged like fish can. But they can stay underwater for a long time.

How long a sea turtle can stay underwater depends on what it is doing. A sea turtle usually swims near the top of the water's surface and breathes every few minutes when it is awake and active. But it might stay underwater for hours when it is resting.

Sea turtles can drown if they get trapped beneath the water's surface for too long. This sometimes happens when they get caught in fishing nets and can't escape.

Leatherback turtles can dive deeper than any other reptiles can. Some scientists believe that this helps them locate the jellyfish they like to eat. They also think these turtles can control their breathing depending on how fast and deep they want to dive.

FUN FACT! Leatherbacks have been recorded diving as deep as 3,937 feet (1,200 m) below the surface.

Leatherbacks are the strongest divers in the turtle family.

CHAPTER 3

Time for Babies

Different sea turtle species start to breed at different ages. Some species may be able to have babies when they are less than 10 years old. Others cannot produce babies until they are older. Green sea turtles do not start breeding until they are between the ages of 25 and 50.

Once she is old enough, a female sea turtle **mates** with a male turtle and lays eggs every one to three years. Although they spend their lives in the sea, sea turtles come onto land to lay their eggs. They drag themselves slowly out of the water and across the sand. The flippers that help them swim so quickly are not designed for moving on land.

The female's **instincts** direct her to return to the beach where she was born to lay her own eggs. A sea turtle might have to travel thousands of miles to get back to the beach where she was born.

Sea turtles leave trails in the sand as they drag themselves across beaches.

A Nesting Instinct

A pregnant sea turtle lays her eggs once she arrives at the spot she's looking for. Then she uses her back flippers to dig a hole in the sand. The hole is usually about 30 inches (76 cm) deep. The eggs fall out of the sea turtle into this sandy hole.

The shell of a sea turtle's egg is spongy. It is not brittle like a chicken's egg. This prevents the egg from breaking when it falls into the hole. A female sea turtle lays between 50 and 200 eggs at a time. A nest of sea turtle eggs is called a clutch. A sea turtle might lay five or more clutches each time she mates. She usually lays these clutches about two weeks apart.

Most sea turtles lay their eggs at night. This gives the eggs a better chance of remaining hidden from predators. Sea turtles know their eggs will make a tasty snack for predators.

Sandy nests help keep a sea turtle's eggs safe from predators.

Hatching Is Hard Work

Which eggs will become female sea turtles? Which will become males? The temperature of the egg during incubation is what makes the difference. Eggs that are in warmer sand usually become females. Eggs in cooler sand are usually male.

A sea turtle egg takes between 45 and 70 days to hatch. A baby turtle uses a special tooth at the edge of its beak to break the shell when it is time to hatch. This is called an egg tooth. It falls out soon after the turtle hatches.

The first job for the turtle hatchling is to get out of its shell. Now it must dig its way out of the sand. This could take as long as a week. The hatchling rests for a few days before it starts this difficult task. It survives during this time by eating the yolk sac inside the egg.

Baby sea turtles are very small when they first hatch.

Making a Run for It

Now the sea turtle has to survive long enough to get to the sea. This is a very dangerous time. Birds, crabs, foxes, and other animals are all threats. Sea turtle hatchlings travel at night to avoid being eaten.

The sea turtles' instincts tell them to travel to the water. The sky above the ocean is lighter than the sky above land. This is how the hatchlings know where to go.

Once a baby sea turtle reaches the ocean, it swims as fast as it can to the safety of deeper water. It might swim for days without stopping. The young turtle will often float along with clumps of seaweed once it gets far enough from shore. It uses this for food and protection. Sea turtles usually stay away from the coast until they grow larger. It is easier for them to protect themselves when they are farther out to sea. If they survive this stage of their life, wild sea turtles may live to be 80 years old.

Hatchlings make their way toward the ocean in large groups.

CHAPTER 4

Sea Turtles Then and Now

Sea turtles have been around for more than 200 million years. This means they shared Earth with the dinosaurs.

One of the oldest known sea turtles was the Proganochelys. This small sea turtle only grew to be about 2 feet (0.6 m) long. Like today's sea turtles, it had a shell and didn't have any teeth. Proganochelys had a unique feature that today's turtles lack. It had spikes on its neck and tail that it used for protection. **Paleontologists** have found **fossils** from this sea turtle in Germany and Thailand.

The Archelon was the biggest sea turtle. It lived about 70 million years ago. The largest Archelon fossil was found in South Dakota. It is 15 feet (4.5 m) long from the edge of its beak to the tip of its tail. That is as big as a car! Scientists believe that the turtle might have weighed as much as 4,500 pounds (2,041 kg).

Some ancient sea turtles were much larger than today's species.

Found Around the World

Today, there are nearly 250 types of turtles. They are found on every continent except Antarctica. Some live in freshwater. Others are found in the ocean. Turtles are also found on land. They may live in the desert, forests, or swamps.

Some turtles are tiny. The smallest are just inches long. Others are huge. The leatherback sea turtle can be taller than a grown man.

All turtles are cold-blooded. This means they need to protect themselves during cold weather. Some turtles hibernate. They slow down their heartbeats and go into a sleeplike state. During this time, they hide away underground, in the water, or in the mud.

All turtles rely on their shells for protection. But sea turtles, unlike other species, cannot pull their head, tail, and legs into their shells. A turtle can never crawl out of its shell. This is because the shell is attached to the turtle's backbone and is part of its body.

Most land turtles are smaller than their cousins in the sea.

Tortoises

Tortoises are also members of the turtle family. They live on land and are often found in dry places such as deserts. A tortoise can store water in its body to help it survive in harsh, dry weather. Tortoises are herbivores. They eat a variety of plant life.

Tortoises have feet instead of flippers. Although their feet are designed for land, tortoises still move very slowly. They also use their feet to help them dig **burrows**. A tortoise can escape to these underground caves when the weather is extremely hot or cold. Burrows can also protect a tortoise when there is a drought or a flood. Some burrows are up to 30 feet (9 m) long.

The Galápagos is the world's largest tortoise. It can weigh up to 550 pounds (250 kg) and be up to 5 feet (1.5 m) long. It also has one of the longest life spans of any animal, often living for over 150 years. This tortoise is only found on the Galápagos Islands off the coast of South America.

The Galápagos tortoise is known for its incredible size.

Terrapins and Snapping Turtles

Terrapins are turtles that divide their time between land and water. They tend to live in water that is **brackish**. This means that it is salty but not as salty as water in the ocean. Terrapins are good swimmers. They have webbed feet instead of flippers. They are carnivores and have strong jaws that can crush the shells of marine animals.

Turtles can also be found in freshwater. One type to avoid is the snapping turtle. Their shells are smaller than their body. This means they can't protect themselves by pulling their head and feet into their shell. Instead, a snapping turtle relies on its hooked jaw for protection. It will bite if it feels threatened.

A snapping turtle will eat almost anything. It is an omnivore, and its diet may include plants, insects, small mammals, and even other turtles. Snapping turtles are usually **nocturnal**.

A snapping turtle's powerful jaws can cause serious injury to its enemies.

CHAPTER 5

Turtles in Trouble

Sea turtles are in danger of becoming **extinct**. Predators kill most hatchlings before they reach adulthood. Humans also cause many problems for turtles.

One big issue is global warming. Many scientists believe that fossil fuels such as gasoline and coal have contributed to warmer temperatures around the world. Higher temperatures can change weather patterns and damage sea turtles' food supplies.

Humans also destroy sea turtles' **habitats**. They clear wild areas to make room for buildings, farms, and roads. This leaves fewer places for turtles to build their nests. It also disrupts the turtles' natural behaviors. Scientists believe that hatchlings are sometimes confused by the light from buildings near their nests. They travel toward the buildings instead of going into the ocean.

The garbage left behind by humans is a danger, too. Sea turtles may think that a plastic bag or piece of Styrofoam is food. They will die if they eat such things.

Turtles often come ashore at the same beaches that people like to use.

Protecting the Sea Turtle

Countries around the world have passed many laws to protect sea turtles. Some of these laws make it illegal to capture or hunt sea turtles. Others require fishermen to use special nets that allow sea turtles to escape.

There are also laws that stop people from clearing wild land or putting up buildings in sea turtle nesting areas. Some places don't allow lights on the beach during sea turtle nesting season. People in some places guard beaches to make sure nothing disturbs turtle nests. Scientists are sometimes hired to help in these efforts. They place screens over sea turtle nests to keep predators out. They keep people away by placing signs and brightly colored ropes around them. Sometimes they even dig up turtle eggs from dangerous areas and rebury them in safer places.

Sea turtles have lived on Earth for hundreds of millions of years. If humans work together, these remarkable animals may survive for many years to come.

Scientists are still working to learn more about the lives of sea turtles.

Words to Know

brackish (BRAK-ish) — water that is somewhat salty

breeds (BREEDZ) — mates and gives birth to young

burrows (BUR-ohz) — tunnels or holes in the ground made or used as a home by an animal

clutch (KLUHCH) — a nest of eggs

continent (KAHN-tuh-nuhnt) — one of the seven large landmasses of the earth

extinct (ik-STINGKT) — no longer found alive

fossils (FOSS-uhlz) — the hardened remains of prehistoric plants and animals

gland (GLAND) — an organ in the body that produces natural chemicals

habitats (HAB-uh-tats) — the places where an animal or a plant is usually found

hatchling (HACH-ling) — a newborn turtle

hibernate (HYE-bur-nate) — to sleep through the winter in order to survive when temperatures are cold and food is hard to find

incubation (ing-kyuh-BAY-shuhn) — the process of keeping eggs warm before they hatch

instincts (IN-stingkts) — natural behaviors or responses

mates (MAYTS) — joins together to produce babies

migrating (MY-grayt-ing) — moving from one area to another

nerve (NURV) — thread that sends messages between the brain and other parts of the body to move and feel

nocturnal (nahk-TUR-nuhl) — active mainly at night

paleontologists (pay-lee-uhn-TAH-luh-jists) — scientists who study fossils and ancient life-forms

predators (PREH-duh-turz) — animals that live by hunting other animals for food

reptiles (REP-tilez) — cold-blooded animals that usually have a backbone and scales and lay eggs

scutes (SCOOTS) — flexible pieces of fingernail-like material that form a turtle's shell

serrated (SEHR-a-ted) — having a jagged edge

species (SPEE-sheez) — one of the groups into which animals and plants of the same genus are divided

submerged (suhb-MURJD) — sunk below the surface of the water

vertebrates (VER-tuh-bruts) — animals that have a backbone

vibrations (vy-BRAY-shunz) — rapid motions back and forth; how a sea turtle can tell that another creature is near

Habitat Map

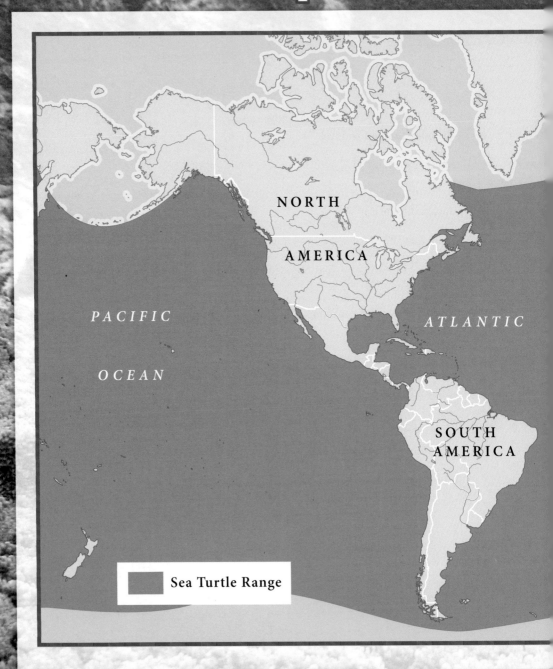

NORTH AMERICA

SOUTH AMERICA

PACIFIC OCEAN

ATLANTIC

Sea Turtle Range

ARCTIC OCEAN

EUROPE

ASIA

AFRICA

INDIAN

OCEAN

OCEAN

PACIFIC

OCEAN

AUSTRALIA

Find Out More

Books

Brennan, Patricia. *Sea Turtles and Other Shelled Reptiles*. Chicago: World Book, Inc., 2002.

Kalman, Bobbie. *Endangered Sea Turtles*. New York: Crabtree Publishing Company, 2004.

Kingston, Anna. *The Life Cycle of a Sea Turtle*. New York: Gareth Stevens Publishing, 2011.

Visit this Scholastic Web site for more information on sea turtles:
www.factsfornow.scholastic.com
Enter the keywords **Sea Turtles**

Index

Page numbers in *italics* indicate a photograph or map.

About the Author

Vicky Franchino has written dozens of books for children and thinks that it's a lot of fun to learn new things. She once saw the tracks of a nesting sea turtle in Costa Rica. It looked like a truck had driven out of the ocean! Vicky lives in Madison, Wisconsin, with her husband and daughters.